# CARIBBEAN
## cooking

**THE AUSTRALIAN Women's Weekly**

Choices

BEERS ..............
SODA ..............
LIME ADE ..............
ORANGE JUICE ..............

COFFEE/TEA ..............
HAM SANDWICH ..............
EGG SANDWICH ..............
CHEESE SANDWICH ..............
CHICKEN SANDWICH ..............
ROAST BEEF SANDWICH ..............
HOT DOG ..............

# contents

Caribbean food brings new culinary meaning to the term "melting pot." Indigenous cooking styles and produce were added to and influenced by recipes and new foods from the British and French, who once colonised the islands, East Indian labourers and African slaves. The blend is a rich and spicy cuisine that is more than the sum of its parts and one that I hope you enjoy reproducing at home.

*Pamela Clark*

Food Director

# the caribbean...

The cooking of the Caribbean is a reflection of the colourful and sometimes tragic history of this remarkable cluster of islands.

Jamaica Tourist Board

The first inhabitants were the Arawaks and the Caribs, descendants of native South Americans who crossed the water from Venezuela and Guyana and settled in the Caribbean long before Christopher Columbus or any other European had sighted the islands. For the Arawaks and Caribs, their new home must have seemed a miracle of abundance and, surrounded by fish, fruit, yams and other vegetables all there for the taking, they thrived.

But in the sixteenth century they found themselves caught in the crossfire of competing colonial interests. The British, French, Portuguese, Spanish and Dutch all sought to seize as many of the Caribbean islands as they could. The islands were a staging post on the great sea journey to the fabulous riches of South America, and every island was a potential base, fortress and treasure hoard.

Although the original inhabitants had grown crops such as corn and beans, they survived largely on the natural plenty all around them. But among the new European colonists were those with a different idea: farming on a giant scale. They brought new animals and plants to the Caribbean: pigs, cattle and sheep appeared on the islands for the first time, as did bananas, coconuts, limes, mangoes, coffee and rice. For the colonists, the Caribbean promised the same instant wealth as the spice islands of the Indies. Europeans, who came as soldiers and sailors to conquer, stayed to build plantations devoted to sugar cane, bananas and other exotic crops. The plantations needed labour, and the great Caribbean tragedy began. Slaves in their millions were shipped in from West Africa, condemned to a short life of misery, poverty and grinding hard work.

Lynn Cole

Jamaica Tourist Board

When the slave trade ended in the nineteenth century, indentured labourers came from India and China to work on the plantations, together with their traders and merchants eager to share the wealth. The great melting pot of Caribbean culture was now complete: the Spanish, French, Africans, Scots, Irish, English, Dutch, Indians and Chinese all brought their music, their sport, their language and their cooking styles, to merge and re-emerge in a riot of colour, sunshine and *joie de vivre*.

# ...and its cooking

A & J's DELI
~ DELICIOUS BAJAN FOOD ~

Every Caribbean cooking style starts with the local ingredients: tropical fruit, chicken, fish and fresh vegetables. To these add spices, yams, peppers and coconut, and the flavour of the Caribbean begins to take shape.

At least one style of Caribbean cooking can now be found all over the world – the barbecue. The word can be traced to French pirates in the Caribbean who gave a particular name to a whole pig roasted on an open fire – *de barbe á queue*, meaning literally "from beard to tail".

The traditional dishes of the Caribbean come from a variety of sources. Jerk Chicken (see page 36) began with the fire-breathing spices necessary to make dried beef or dried venison – jerky to the early European sailors – more edible on long sea voyages. The same sailors brought salt cod with them – salting was another way of preserving food. Today, salt cod is treated as a delicacy. Stamp and Go (see page 8), as spicy fishcakes are called, was sold from seaside stalls and came wrapped in paper stamped with the word "paid" – you paid and off you went.

The extensive use of spices makes Caribbean food lively and different and, like so many cooking traditions, owes its beginning to pure necessity. African slaves grew tired of the boring and basic food they were given, and made it palatable with a hefty sprinkling of locally grown spices. But, most of all, Caribbean food is about fresh ingredients, freshly cooked. It is our great good fortune today that even the most exotic ingredients can be found in supermarkets all around the world. We no longer have to travel to Trinidad or Jamaica to share the joy of fresh mango or pineapple, or to Havana to mix a rum cocktail. The flavours of the Caribbean have been brought to us, wherever we live. In this book we have tried to use only those ingredients that are easily obtainable. If an ingredient is hard to find, we've tried to offer a substitute.

So imagine yourself on a sunny beach, with the sparkling Caribbean lapping gently on the sand, a steel band playing softly in the distance and the glorious tastes of the tropics surrounding you. If you can't make a real-life journey to the Caribbean, you can still sample the flavours and delights at home, using this book.

*Tasty nibbles are sold from roadside or seaside stalls throughout the Caribbean. Most of the traditional snacks on the following pages can be served either hot or cold.*

# coconut prawns

preparation time 25 minutes (plus marinating time) ✿ cooking time 4 minutes

16 uncooked jumbo prawns (800g)
2 tablespoons lime juice
1 tablespoon dry white wine
4 cloves garlic, crushed
1/2 teaspoon salt
1/4 teaspoon freshly ground black pepper
1 cup (90g) desiccated coconut
2 tablespoons finely chopped
   fresh coriander leaves
2 tablespoons plain flour
2 eggs, beaten lightly
vegetable oil, for deep-frying
2 limes, cut into wedges

1 Shell and devein prawns, leaving tails intact.

2 Combine juice, wine, garlic, salt and pepper in medium bowl, add prawns; stir to coat prawns in marinade. Cover; refrigerate 1 hour.

3 Combine coconut and coriander in medium shallow dish.

4 Remove prawns from marinade, pat dry with paper towel; discard marinade. Place flour in strong plastic bag, add prawns to bag; shake to coat. Remove prawns; shake off excess flour. Dip prawns in egg, then roll in coconut mixture until coated all over; press on coconut.

5 Heat oil in large saucepan; deep-fry prawns, in batches, about 1 minute or until golden brown.

6 Serve hot with lime wedges.

SERVES 4

*Jamaica Tourist Board*

# stamp and go
## (saltfish cakes)

preparation time 20 minutes (plus soaking time) ✿ cooking time 45 minutes

300g salt cod
pinch saffron threads
1 tablespoon water
1 egg, beaten lightly
1/3 cup (80ml) milk
1 1/3 cups (200g) plain flour
2 teaspoons baking powder
1/2 teaspoon salt
1/4 teaspoon freshly ground
    black pepper
2 tablespoons finely chopped
    spring onion
2 cloves garlic, crushed
1 small fresh red chilli, chopped finely
sunflower oil, for shallow-frying

1 Soak fish 12 hours or overnight in large bowl of cold water.

2 Drain fish, rinse under cold water; place in large saucepan, cover with cold water. Bring to a boil; simmer gently, uncovered, 20-25 minutes. Drain; cool. Remove and discard skin and bones; flake flesh. Set aside.

3 In small bowl, soak saffron in the water about 2 minutes. Add egg and milk; stir to combine.

4 Sift flour and baking powder into large bowl, add salt and black pepper; mix well. Stir in flaked fish, onion, garlic and chilli.

5 Add saffron mixture, in batches, stirring, until batter is smooth.

6 Heat 2 tablespoons of the oil in large frying pan; cook level tablespoons of batter, in batches, about 2 minutes each side or until golden brown. Add more oil to pan between batches. Serve hot or cold.

SERVES 6 (MAKES 24)

# caribbean crisps

preparation time 10 minutes ✿ cooking time 15 minutes

*No need to think of crisps as made only from potatoes. You can produce unusual and delicious crisps to accompany your drinks with these tropical ingredients.*

1 small red sweet potato (250g)
1 plantain
vegetable oil, for deep-frying
salt, to serve

1 Peel potato and plantain; slice as thinly as possible.

2 Heat oil in large deep saucepan.

3 Deep-fry potato and plantain, in batches, 1-2 minutes or until crisp. Remove from oil with slotted spoon; drain crisps on paper towel, cool.

4 Sprinkle crisps with salt to serve.

SERVES 4

tips Plantain skins can be hard to remove cleanly. Try cutting off the ends with a sharp knife, then make five or six slits along the length of the skin. The strips of skin should now peel away.

If you prefer, you could substitute yam and green banana for the sweet potato and plantain.

# chilli crab-filled capsicums

preparation time 20 minutes ✿ cooking time 5 minutes

*This dish can give out just a hint of chilli from the red chillies, or be turned into a
really fiery starter with the addition of 1 tablespoon of chilli sauce.*

3 large green capsicums (1kg)
3 cups (510g) cooked crab meat
4 hard-boiled eggs, chopped finely
2 small fresh red chillies, seeded,
  chopped finely
2 tablespoons finely chopped
  spring onions
1 tablespoon finely chopped
  fresh flat-leaf parsley
2 teaspoons finely grated lemon rind
1/3 cup (80ml) lemon juice
1 cup (300g) mayonnaise
1/2 cup (140g) plain yogurt

1 Halve capsicums lengthways, remove seeds and membranes.
  Place capsicum halves in large saucepan of cold water, bring to a
  boil; simmer gently, uncovered, 2 minutes. Drain capsicum, rinse
  immediately in cold water; pat dry with paper towel.

2 Combine crab, egg, chilli, onion, parsley, rind, juice, mayonnaise and
  yogurt in large bowl.

3 To serve, spoon crab mixture into capsicum halves.

SERVES 6

# spinach pies

1²/3 cups (250g) plain flour
¹/2 teaspoon salt
60g butter
1 cup (250ml) cold water
1 teaspoon lemon juice
30g butter, extra
1 small brown onion (80g),
   chopped finely
100g finely chopped spinach
¹/2 teaspoon freshly grated nutmeg
¹/4 teaspoon freshly ground black pepper
¹/4 cup (40g) pine nuts, toasted

1 Sift flour and salt into large bowl. Using fingertips, rub butter into flour mixture. Using knife, stir in combined water and juice. Roll dough into ball; divide in half.

2 Roll one dough portion on floured surface. Using 7mm cutter, cut 12 rounds from dough. Repeat with remaining portion. Line greased holes of 12-hole (30ml) patty tin with 12 pastry rounds.

3 Preheat oven to moderately hot.

4 Melt extra butter in medium saucepan, add onion; cook until onion is soft. Stir in spinach; cook 5 minutes. Add nutmeg, pepper and pine nuts; stir to combine.

5 Fill pastry rounds in patty tin with even quantities of spinach mixture. Seal spinach pies with remaining pastry rounds. Using fork, prick top of each pie twice.

6 Bake pies, uncovered, in moderately hot oven 20 minutes or until golden brown. Serve hot or cold.

SERVES 4

tip Frozen spinach can be used instead of fresh spinach, if you prefer.

# escovitch

preparation time 25 minutes ✿ cooking time 25 minutes (plus cooling time)

*Escovitch was originally Portuguese, but is now found in dozens of variations around the Caribbean islands. This is one of the most popular versions. You can serve it on individual plates, but most people prefer to put the whole serving dish in the centre of the table and allow their guests to make their selection with toothpicks.*

2 medium brown onions (300g), sliced thinly
2 cloves garlic, sliced thinly
2 medium carrots (240g), cut into 1cm slices
1 medium green capsicum (200g), cut into 1cm pieces
1 bouquet garni
1/2 cup (125ml) white wine vinegar
2 tablespoons olive oil
12 green peppercorns
1 teaspoon salt
1 cup (250ml) cold water
500g red snapper fillets

1 Place onion, garlic, carrot, capsicum, bouquet garni, vinegar, 1 tablespoon of the oil, peppercorns, salt and the water in large saucepan. Bring to a boil; simmer gently, uncovered, 15 minutes.

2 Heat remaining oil in large frying pan; cook fish, in batches, 3 minutes on each side or until golden. Place fish on serving plate; cut fillets into bite-size pieces.

3 Remove bouquet garni from pan, discard. Pour vegetable mixture over fish; allow to cool before serving.

SERVES 4

*Caribbean soup can be anything from a light and delicious cold starter to a hearty meal of fish, meat or vegetables. We have given you some basic recipes for traditional soups, most of which can be varied to suit your taste – so feel free to add any suitable ingredients that take your fancy.*

# fish and sweet potato chowder

preparation time 15 minutes ✿ cooking time 40 minutes

1 tablespoon olive oil
1 small brown onion (80g),
    chopped coarsely
1 medium red sweet potato (400g),
    cut into 2cm pieces
1 medium carrot (120g),
    chopped coarsely
1.5 litres (6 cups) fish stock
200g firm white fish fillets, cut into
    2cm pieces
1 teaspoon finely chopped fresh oregano
1/2 teaspoon freshly grated nutmeg
1/2 cup (125ml) single cream

1  Heat oil in medium saucepan, add onion; cook until onion is soft. Add sweet potato and carrot; cook, stirring, 2 minutes.

2  Add stock, bring to a boil; simmer gently, covered, 20 minutes or until sweet potato is cooked.

3  Blend or process stock and vegetables until smooth.

4  Return mixture to same pan; add fish, oregano and nutmeg. Bring to a boil; simmer, covered, 5 minutes or until fish is cooked.

5  Stir in cream; simmer gently, stirring, until soup is heated through – do not boil.

6  Serve chowder topped with coriander, if desired.

SERVES 4

tip  You can substitute 1/2 teaspoon dried oregano for the fresh oregano.

Lynn Cole

# pumpkin soup

preparation time 15 minutes ✿ cooking time 35 minutes

90g butter
1 large brown onion (200g),
   chopped coarsely
2 cloves garlic, chopped coarsely
1 teaspoon curry powder
2 medium potatoes (400g),
   chopped coarsely
400g coarsely chopped pumpkin
3 cups (750ml) chicken stock
1 teaspoon salt
1/2 teaspoon freshly ground
   black pepper
1 tablespoon finely chopped
   fresh flat-leaf parsley
1 cup (250ml) coconut milk
1/2 small leek (100g), sliced finely
1/3 cup (80g) sour cream

1  Melt 2 tablespoons of the butter in large, heavy-based saucepan. Add onion and garlic; cook until onion is soft. Add curry powder; cook, stirring, 1 minute. Add potato and pumpkin; cook, stirring, 1 minute or until vegetables are coated in butter.

2  Add stock, salt, pepper, parsley and, if necessary, enough water to just cover vegetables. Bring to a boil; simmer, covered, 20 minutes or until vegetables are cooked through.

3  Blend or process vegetable mixture until smooth. Return mixture to pan, stir in coconut milk; simmer until soup is heated through.

4  Meanwhile, melt remaining butter in small frying pan, add leek; cook until leek is soft.

5  Serve soup with a swirl of sour cream in each bowl; top with leek.

SERVES 4

tips  This soup can also be served cold. Allow the soup to cool to room temperature and refrigerate for at least 1 hour. Instead of leek, top cold soup with 1 tablespoon finely chopped fresh chives.

If you prefer, use plain yogurt in place of the sour cream.

# caribbean
# chicken hotpot

*This hearty soup is definitely a main meal! Our recipe uses chicken, but you can vary the dish by using lamb or beef, or even leaving meat out altogether. Stretch the soup by adding more stock. Or make it even more filling by adding other vegetables of your choice.*

2 tablespoons plain flour
1 teaspoon salt
$1/2$ teaspoon freshly ground black pepper
8 chicken thighs (1.8kg), skinned, boned, cut into bite-size pieces
2 tablespoons olive oil
1 large brown onion (200g), chopped finely
2 cloves garlic, crushed
1 small red sweet potato (250g), cut into 2cm pieces
2 medium carrots (240g), sliced
2 trimmed sticks celery (150g), chopped finely
2 medium green bananas (400g), peeled, sliced
$1/4$ cup (50g) red lentils
1.5 litres (6 cups) chicken stock
1 teaspoon chilli sauce
1 bouquet garni
150g pasta

1  Combine flour, half of the salt and half of the pepper in shallow dish. Toss chicken in flour, shake off excess.

2  Heat oil in large saucepan; cook chicken, in batches, about 5 minutes or until brown all over. Set aside.

3  Add onion and garlic to same pan; cook until onion is soft. Add potato, carrot and celery; cook, stirring, 2 minutes or until vegetables are lightly coated with oil.

4  Add banana, lentils, chicken, stock, remaining salt and pepper, chilli sauce and bouquet garni; bring to a boil, stirring. Reduce heat; simmer gently, covered, 15 minutes.

5  Add pasta; bring to a boil, stirring. Simmer, covered, 10 minutes. Remove and discard bouquet garni.

6  Serve soup sprinkled with fresh parsley, if desired.

SERVES 4

tip  Penne, macaroni or shell pasta are all suitable for this recipe.

# green pea soup

preparation time 20 minutes ✿ cooking time 40 minutes

50g butter
3 shallots, chopped finely
1 medium red sweet potato (400g),
    cut into 1cm pieces
1 medium red capsicum (200g),
    chopped finely
2 medium tomatoes (380g), peeled,
    seeded, chopped finely
2 cups (500ml) chicken stock
3 cups (370g) frozen peas
1¹/4 cups (210g) chopped
    cooked chicken
¹/2 cup (125ml) single cream
2 tablespoons finely chopped
    fresh mint leaves

1  Melt butter in medium saucepan, add shallot; cook until shallot is soft. Add potato and capsicum; cook, stirring, 1 minute. Add tomato; cook, stirring, 1 minute.

2  Add stock and peas, bring to a boil; simmer, uncovered, 20 minutes. The potato and peas should become mushy, but not lose their shape.

3  Add chicken; simmer, uncovered, 5 minutes. Stir in cream; simmer until soup is heated through – do not boil.

4  If desired, add a little salt and freshly ground black pepper. Serve soup sprinkled with mint.

SERVES 4

Lynn Cole

# cream of coconut and banana soup

preparation time 15 minutes ✿ cooking time 35 minutes

4 medium green bananas (740g)
2 tablespoons olive oil
1 medium brown onion (150g), chopped coarsely
1 clove garlic, crushed
2 cups (500ml) chicken stock
1 cup (250ml) coconut milk

1 Preheat oven to moderate.

2 Place whole bananas on oven tray; bake in moderate oven 25 minutes or until cooked. Remove and discard skins; reserve bananas.

3 Heat oil in medium saucepan; cook onion and garlic until onion is soft.

4 Add stock and coconut milk, bring to a boil; simmer gently, covered, 5 minutes.

5 Blend or process stock mixture and bananas until pureed. Return mixture to same pan; simmer until soup is heated through.

6 Serve soup topped with coriander, if desired.

SERVES 4

tip This soup is also delicious served cold. To serve cold, allow the soup to cool to room temperature after cooking, then refrigerate for at least 1 hour.

# callaloo

preparation time 20 minutes (plus marinating time) ✿ cooking time 55 minutes

*Callaloo is a traditional soup from the island of Barbados.*

**30g butter**
**1 medium brown onion (150g), chopped finely**
**2 cloves garlic, crushed**
**150g okra, trimmed, cut into 1cm slices**
**2 teaspoons fresh thyme leaves**
**300g spinach leaves, trimmed, chopped finely**
**2 cups (500ml) chicken stock**
**1 cup (250ml) coconut milk**
**1/2 teaspoon salt**
**1/4 teaspoon freshly ground black pepper**
**200g fresh crab meat**
**1 teaspoon chilli sauce**
**1 tablespoon finely chopped chives**

1 Melt butter in large saucepan, add onion and garlic; cook gently, until onion is soft.

2 Add okra and thyme to onion mixture; cook gently, stirring, 5 minutes. Add spinach; cook, stirring, 3 minutes or until spinach has wilted.

3 Pour in stock and coconut milk. Add salt and pepper; bring to a boil, stirring. Simmer gently, covered, 30 minutes.

4 Add crab meat and sauce; simmer gently, covered, stirring occasionally, 5 minutes.

5 Serve soup sprinkled with chives.

SERVES 4

**tip** If you prefer, fresh ingredients can be replaced with alternatives: use frozen spinach instead of fresh spinach, 1 teaspoon dried thyme in place of the fresh thyme, and tinned or frozen crab instead of fresh crab meat.

There are as many chicken dishes in the Caribbean as there are cooks. Every household has its chicken speciality. The recipes that follow are a good example of the way Caribbean cooks have taken inspiration from a variety of cooking styles – curries from India, stir-fries from China, roasts from England – and given them their unique tropical twist.

# devilled chicken

preparation time 15 minutes ❀ cooking time 55 minutes

30g butter
1 large brown onion (200g),
   chopped finely
2 cloves garlic, crushed
2 tablespoons tomato sauce
1 tablespoon Worcestershire sauce
1 tablespoon French mustard
2 tablespoons mango chutney
$^1/_2$ teaspoon ground allspice
$^1/_2$ teaspoon salt
$^1/_2$ teaspoon freshly ground black pepper
8 chicken thighs (1.8kg)

1 Melt butter in medium saucepan, add onion and garlic; cook until onion is soft.

2 Add sauces, mustard, chutney, allspice, salt and pepper, stir well; simmer, covered, 5 minutes.

3 Preheat oven to moderate.

4 Place chicken, skin-side up, in oiled baking dish; pour sauce mixture over top, completely covering chicken with mixture.

5 Bake chicken, uncovered, in moderate oven 45 minutes, occasionally basting with chicken juices.

6 Serve with a tomato and chickpea salad, if desired.

SERVES 4

Jamaica Tourist Board

# sweet chicken stew

preparation time 25 minutes (plus marinating time) ✿ cooking time 1 hour

*The key to this recipe is the caramel coating given to the chicken when it is browned
in the oil-and-sugar mixture.*

1 medium brown onion (150g),
   chopped finely
3 medium tomatoes (470g),
   chopped finely
1 trimmed stick celery (75g),
   chopped finely
1 tablespoon finely chopped spring onion
3 tablespoons finely chopped
   fresh flat-leaf parsley
2 cloves garlic, crushed
1 teaspoon fresh thyme leaves
1 tablespoon lime juice
2 tablespoons sweet chilli sauce
$1/2$ teaspoon salt
$1/2$ teaspoon freshly ground black pepper
8 chicken drumsticks (1.2kg), skinned
2 tablespoons olive oil
2 tablespoons dark brown sugar
2 cups (500ml) chicken stock
1 tablespoon tomato paste
2 medium carrots (240g),
   cut into 1cm slices
1 lime, cut into wedges

1 Combine brown onion, tomato, celery, spring onion, parsley, garlic, thyme, juice, sauce, salt and pepper in large bowl. Add chicken drumsticks, mix well to coat, cover; refrigerate overnight.

2 Heat oil in large saucepan, add sugar; cook until mixture begins to bubble. Drain chicken; reserve marinade. Cook chicken, in batches, rolling it in sugar mixture, until browned all over and coated in sugar mixture.

3 Add stock to same pan; stir to combine stock and pan juices. Add tomato paste and reserved marinade, stir. Add chicken and carrot; simmer, covered, 45 minutes or until chicken is cooked through, turning chicken at least once during cooking.

4 Remove lid from pan, bring to a boil; simmer, uncovered, until liquid has reduced by about half, taking care not to let the contents burn or stick to the bottom of the pan.

5 Serve with wedges of lime.

SERVES 4

# jamaican chicken and ham

preparation time 25 minutes ✿ cooking time 1 hour

*This recipe is a Jamaican adaptation of a classic Indian curry. It makes good use of Caribbean ingredients such as mango and green banana.*

50g butter
4 chicken breast fillets (700g), cut into 3cm pieces
1 medium brown onion (150g), chopped finely
1 tablespoon curry powder
1/2 teaspoon ground cinnamon
1/2 teaspoon ground cardamom
1/2 teaspoon mace
100g leg ham, diced
1 large apple (200g), peeled, cored, chopped coarsely
1 medium green banana (200g), sliced
1 medium mango (430g), seeded, chopped coarsely
2 large tomatoes (500g), peeled, seeded, chopped coarsely
1 1/4 cups (310ml) coconut milk
1 tablespoon lemon juice
1/2 teaspoon salt
1/2 cup (140g) plain yogurt

1 Melt butter in large heavy-based saucepan; cook chicken, in batches, until chicken starts to brown. Return all of the chicken to pan, add onion; cook until onion is soft.

2 Add curry powder, cinnamon, cardamom and mace; cook, stirring, 1 minute. Add ham, apple, banana, mango, tomato, coconut milk, juice and salt; if necessary, add a little water so that liquid just covers chicken. Stir well; simmer, covered, stirring occasionally, 40 minutes or until chicken is cooked through.

3 Add yogurt; stir until heated through – do not boil. Serve with plain boiled rice, if desired.

SERVES 4

tip If you prefer, use eight chicken thighs, skinned, boned and diced, in place of the chicken breasts.

# tobago
# chicken hotpot

75g butter
1 chicken (1.5kg), cut into eight pieces
2 medium brown onions (300g), sliced finely
2 cloves garlic, sliced finely
1 tablespoon curry powder
1 fresh red chilli, seeded, chopped finely
$1/2$ teaspoon saffron threads
1 cup (250ml) coconut milk
$1/2$ teaspoon salt
2 cups (500ml) water, approximately

1  Melt butter in large flameproof baking dish; cook chicken, in batches, 5 minutes or until golden brown all over. Set aside.

2  In same dish, cook onion and garlic until onion is soft and just beginning to brown. Add curry powder, chilli and saffron; cook, stirring, 1 minute.

3  Return chicken to dish, add half of the coconut milk, salt and just enough cold water to cover chicken pieces; bring to a boil. Reduce heat; simmer, covered, 40 minutes. Add remaining coconut milk; cook until heated through.

SERVES 4

**serving suggestion** Tobago chicken hotpot is traditionally served with plain boiled rice and side dishes such as sliced banana, chopped tomato, chopped red onion and plain yogurt.

# jerk chicken

preparation time 15 minutes (plus marinating time) ✿ cooking time 55 minutes

*Traditional Caribbean jerk dishes began with dried meat, usually beef (or jerky, as it was known to sailors). In the days before refrigeration, meats – especially beef and venison – were cut into strips and dried in the sun to preserve them for long sea voyages. The meat was none too appetising at meal time, so the sailors made it more palatable by adding plenty of powerful spices. Now jerk dishes are no longer associated with dried meat, but instead refer to the fiery seasonings that give them their special flavour.*

2 tablespoons plain yogurt
1 tablespoon chilli sauce
1 teaspoon finely grated lime rind
2 tablespoons lime juice
1 teaspoon ground allspice
1/2 teaspoon salt
1/2 teaspoon freshly ground black pepper
1 medium brown onion (150g),
   chopped coarsely
2 cloves garlic, chopped coarsely
1 tablespoon grated fresh ginger root
1 tablespoon coarsely chopped
   fresh coriander leaves
1 tablespoon coarse-grain mustard
2 tablespoons light brown sugar
1 tablespoon olive oil
4 chicken breast fillets (700g)

1 Blend or process yogurt, sauce, rind, juice, allspice, salt, pepper, brown onion, garlic, ginger, coriander, mustard, sugar and oil until smooth. Place marinade in baking dish. Add chicken, mix well to coat, cover; refrigerate 1 hour.

2 Preheat oven to moderate.

3 Bake chicken, uncovered, in moderate oven 50 minutes, turning at least once.

4 Remove chicken from oven, place under hot grill; cook about 2 minutes each side or until browned.

SERVES 4

tip This dish can also be cooked on a barbecue, in a grill pan or under the griller. For grilling or barbecuing, use a little extra oil in the marinade.

*Jamaica Tourist Board*

# chicken with caribbean stuffing

preparation time 20 minutes ✿ cooking time 1 hour 10 minutes

1/2 cup cooked white medium–grain rice
2 teaspoons finely grated lime rind
4 tablespoons lime juice
1/4 teaspoon ground nutmeg
1/2 teaspoon salt
1/4 teaspoon freshly ground black pepper
1 medium banana (200g), sliced thickly
230g tinned pineapple chunks, drained
1 tablespoon finely chopped fresh
    coriander leaves
1 tablespoon olive oil
1 chicken (1.5kg)
50g butter
1 cup (250ml) chicken stock
1 teaspoon light brown sugar
1 tablespoon dark rum

1 Combine rice, rind, juice, nutmeg, salt, pepper, banana, pineapple, coriander and oil in medium bowl. Stuff chicken with the mixture.

2 Preheat oven to moderate.

3 Lightly grease baking dish with a little of the butter; smear remaining butter all over chicken.

4 Roast chicken, uncovered, in moderate oven 1 hour or until cooked through, basting occasionally. Remove chicken from dish; set aside in warm place.

5 Skim off any excess fat from pan juices in baking dish; discard fat. Add stock; stir into pan juices. Pour stock mixture into small saucepan, add sugar; bring to a boil. Reduce heat; simmer, uncovered, until liquid has reduced by half.

6 Heat rum until almost boiling, sprinkle over chicken; set chicken alight.

7 Serve chicken with reduced sauce.

SERVES 4

tip This stuffing works equally well with turkey, though you will need larger quantities. It makes an exotic alternative to the traditional Christmas dinner.

# tobago chicken stir-fry

preparation time 25 minutes (plus marinating time) ✿ cooking time 20 minutes

1/4 cup (60ml) soy sauce
1 tablespoon dark rum
1 tablespoon cornflour
1 teaspoon light brown sugar
1 teaspoon ground allspice
1 teaspoon ground ginger
1/2 teaspoon salt
1/4 teaspoon cayenne pepper
4 chicken breast fillets (700g),
    cut into 2cm strips
2 tablespoons vegetable oil
1 medium brown onion (150g),
    chopped coarsely
2 cloves garlic, sliced thinly
100g button mushrooms, sliced thickly
1 medium red capsicum (200g),
    cut into 1cm strips
1 medium carrot (120g), peeled,
    shaved into strips
200g mangetout
400g tin pineapple chunks, drained
100g unsalted roasted cashew nuts

1 Combine sauce, rum, cornflour, sugar, spices, salt and cayenne pepper in large bowl; stir well. Add chicken, stir to coat chicken, cover; refrigerate at least 1 hour.

2 Drain chicken; discard marinade. Heat oil in wok or large frying pan. Add chicken to wok; cook, in batches, until chicken is brown and cooked through. Set aside.

3 Add onion, garlic, mushrooms, capsicum and carrot to wok; stir-fry 5 minutes or until vegetables are tender.

4 Add mangetout, pineapple, cashew nuts and chicken; stir-fry until heated through.

SERVES 4

Lynn Cole

# chicken with chickpeas and rice

preparation time 15 minutes ✿ cooking time 40 minutes

*This variation on the Spanish dish paella uses tropical ingredients such as coconut. If you wish, you can add typical paella ingredients such as mussels, prawns and salt pork. Salt pork should be added with the chicken. Uncooked mussels can be added at the last minute, when the rice is almost cooked. Mussels are ready when the shells open – discard any that do not open. Cooked prawns should also be added at the last minute, and simply heated through with the rice and chicken.*

50g butter
8 chicken drumsticks (1.2kg)
1 medium brown onion (150g),
   chopped finely
2 cloves garlic, sliced finely
1 fresh red chilli, seeded,
   chopped finely
1 medium red capsicum (200g),
   cut into 1.5cm pieces
1 cup (200g) white long-grain rice
2 tablespoons desiccated coconut
1¼ cups (310ml) coconut milk
1 tablespoon fresh thyme leaves
400g tin chickpeas, drained
½ teaspoon saffron threads
2 cups (500ml) chicken stock
1 tablespoon finely chopped
   spring onions
1 lemon, cut into wedges

1 Melt butter in large heavy-based frying pan or paella pan. Add chicken; cook 5 minutes or until chicken is browned all over.

2 Add brown onion, garlic, chilli and capsicum to pan; cook until onion is soft. Add rice; cook 2 minutes, stirring constantly, until rice is coated in butter. Add coconut, coconut milk, thyme and chickpeas, stirring well.

3 Stir saffron into stock; add half of the liquid to pan. Bring to a boil, reduce heat; simmer gently, uncovered, 20 minutes or until rice is cooked, adding more stock, a little at a time, as rice absorbs liquid. If you run out of stock, add a little water.

4 Serve topped with spring onion and lemon wedges.

SERVES 4

# haiti chicken casserole

preparation time 20 minutes ✿ cooking time 1 hour 15 minutes

2 tablespoons olive oil
8 chicken thighs (1.8kg)
1 large brown onion (200g), sliced finely
2 cloves garlic, sliced finely
1 medium red capsicum (200g), cut into 1cm strips
1 medium green capsicum (200g), cut into 1cm strips
1 medium yellow capsicum (200g), cut into 1cm strips
1 tablespoon plain flour
2 cups (500ml) chicken stock
1 teaspoon fresh thyme leaves
1 bay leaf
2 tablespoons sweet chilli sauce
1 teaspoon salt
$1/2$ teaspoon freshly ground black pepper
2 large tomatoes (500g), peeled, sliced thickly

1  Heat oil in large heavy-based saucepan. Add chicken; cook until chicken is well browned. Set aside.

2  In same pan, cook onion, garlic and capsicums until onion is soft. Add flour; cook, stirring constantly, 2 minutes or until flour is spread evenly and lightly cooked.

3  Add stock, bring to a boil; boil, uncovered, stirring constantly, until mixture has slightly thickened.

4  Add thyme, bay leaf, sauce, salt, black pepper, tomato and chicken to pan. The chicken pieces should be just covered by stock. If not, add a little water. Bring to a boil, reduce heat; simmer, covered, 45 minutes. Remove and discard bay leaf.

5  Serve casserole with plain boiled rice and top with a sprig of thyme, if desired.

SERVES 4

West Indian cooks generally concentrate on lamb and pork, though goat is also popular
(and, if you can find it, can be substituted for lamb in all the recipes that follow). Beef dishes
are more common in Cuba and the other Hispanic islands of the Caribbean. The meat dishes we
have chosen reflect the wide variety of cooking styles and ingredients used by Caribbean cooks.

# spiced lamb chops

preparation time 10 minutes (plus marinating time) ✿ cooking time 50 minutes

1¼ cups (310ml) orange juice
2 tablespoons aniseed, crushed
1 teaspoon garam masala
1 fresh red chilli, seeded, chopped finely
1 tablespoon honey
½ teaspoon salt
2 tablespoons dark rum
8 thickly cut lamb loin chops (1.4kg)

1 Combine juice, aniseed, garam masala, chilli, honey, salt and rum in baking dish. Add lamb; turn to coat with marinade. Cover; refrigerate at least 1 hour, turning once.

2 Preheat oven to moderate.

3 Roast lamb, uncovered, in moderate oven 45 minutes, basting frequently. Remove lamb from dish; set aside in warm place.

4 Pour marinade into small saucepan, bring to a boil; boil, uncovered, until sauce has reduced by about half.

5 Pour sauce over lamb to serve.

SERVES 4

**serving suggestion** This dish is excellent accompanied by a cucumber and yogurt salad.

Debbie Quick

# char-grilled pork chops with herbs

preparation time 15 minutes ✿ cooking time 16 minutes

1 tablespoon coarsely chopped
  fresh rosemary
2 teaspoons fresh thyme leaves
2 tablespoons coarsely chopped
  fresh flat-leaf parsley
3 cloves garlic
1/2 teaspoon salt
1/2 teaspoon freshly ground black pepper
2 tablespoons olive oil
4 pork loin chops (800g)

1 Blend or process herbs, garlic, salt, pepper and oil until ingredients are well chopped and mixed.

2 Spread half of the herb mixture evenly on one side of the chops. Place chops, herbed-side down, in grill pan (or on barbecue); cook 8 minutes. Spread remaining herb mixture evenly on chops, turn chops; cook 8 minutes.

3 Serve with a mango or other fruit salsa, if desired.

SERVES 4

tip The pork chops can also be cooked under a grill. Cook chops herbed-side up in this case so that the herbed side faces the heat.

*Jamaica Tourist Board*

# minted roast lamb

preparation time 25 minutes ✿ cooking time 1 hour 45 minutes

2 medium brown onions (300g), chopped coarsely
2 cups loosely packed fresh mint leaves
1 teaspoon finely grated lime rind
2 tablespoons lime juice
2 green chillies, seeded
1 tablespoon allspice, crushed
1 leg lamb (approximately 2kg)
1 teaspoon salt
1 tablespoon soy sauce
1/4 cup (90g) honey
1/2 cup (125ml) lamb stock

1 Blend or process onion, mint, rind, juice, chilli and allspice until smooth. Using a sharp knife, make 20-30 deep slits all over lamb; poke as much onion mixture into slits as possible, spread remaining mixture over lamb.

2 Preheat oven to moderately slow.

3 Place lamb in baking dish, fat-side up; sprinkle salt over lamb.

4 Roast lamb, uncovered, in moderately slow 1 hour 40 minutes, basting frequently. Remove lamb from dish; set aside in warm place.

5 Skim off any excess fat from pan juices in baking dish; discard fat. Add soy sauce, honey and stock; stir into pan juices. Pour stock mixture into small saucepan, bring to a boil; boil, uncovered, until sauce has reduced by half.

6 Serve lamb with sauce.

SERVES 6

**serving suggestion** Serve this dish as a wonderful change from the usual Sunday roast, with baked sweet potatoes and crisp fried okra.

# lamb and lentil curry

preparation time 25 minutes ✿ cooking time 1 hour 15 minutes

1 tablespoon plain flour
1 tablespoon curry powder
1/4 teaspoon chilli powder
1 teaspoon ground ginger
1/2 teaspoon salt
1/2 teaspoon freshly ground
   black pepper
50g butter
1kg trimmed diced lamb
1 large brown onion (200g),
   chopped coarsely
2 cloves garlic, crushed
1 medium red capsicum (200g),
   seeded, cut into 1cm squares
400g tin tomatoes, chopped coarsely
2 cups (500ml) lamb stock
1 1/4 cup (250g) brown lentils,
   rinsed and drained
1/2 cup (125ml) coconut milk

1 Combine flour, powders, ginger, salt and black pepper in small bowl.

2 Melt butter in large heavy-based saucepan; cook lamb, in batches, until browned all over. Set aside.

3 Add onion, garlic and capsicum to same pan; cook until onion is soft and just beginning to brown. Add curry mixture, stir well; cook, stirring, 1 minute.

4 Add undrained tomatoes and stock, stir well. Add lamb, lentils and coconut milk; simmer gently, covered, stirring occasionally, 1 hour or until lamb and lentils are cooked.

SERVES 4

**serving suggestion** This dish can be served with plain boiled rice or on its own. Place bowls of mango chutney, chopped banana, chopped tomato, desiccated coconut and plain yogurt on the table as extra accompaniments.

# cuban char-grilled lamb with onion and capsicum

preparation time 15 minutes (plus marinating time) ✿ cooking time 30 minutes

4 tablespoons finely chopped
    fresh flat-leaf parsley
1 tablespoon sweet paprika
4 cloves garlic, crushed
1 teaspoon salt
1/4 cup (60ml) olive oil
8 lamb loin chops (1kg)
2 medium red onions (340g),
    sliced thinly
2 medium green capsicums (400g),
    cut into 1cm strips
1 medium yellow capsicum (200g),
    cut into 1cm strips
2 tablespoons dry white wine

1  Blend or process parsley, paprika, garlic, salt and 1 tablespoon of the oil until mixture forms a paste. Spread paste over lamb until coated, cover; refrigerate 1 hour.

2  Heat remaining oil in large saucepan; cook onion, stirring, until soft. Add capsicums; cook 2 minutes.

3  Add wine, cover; simmer gently, stirring occasionally, 20 minutes.

4  Meanwhile, cook lamb in grill pan (or on barbecue or under grill) until cooked through.

5  Serve lamb with onion and capsicum, accompanied by mashed sweet potato and a green salad, if desired.

SERVES 4

55

# jerk pork chops

preparation time 15 minutes (plus marinating time)
cooking time 20 minutes

2 fresh red chillies, seeded, chopped finely
2 teaspoons finely grated lime rind
1/3 cup (80ml) lime juice
1 teaspoon ground cinnamon
1 teaspoon ground nutmeg
2 tablespoons ground allspice
1 tablespoon chilli sauce
2 cloves garlic, crushed
4 pork loin chops (800g)

1 Combine chillies, rind, juice, spices, sauce and garlic in small bowl; mix well. Spread mixture over both sides of chops, adding a little olive oil to mixture if it is too dry to spread. Cover; refrigerate 1 hour or overnight.

2 Cook chops on barbecue (or in grill pan or under grill) 10 minutes each side or until cooked through. Serve with grilled lime pieces, if desired.

SERVES 4

tip This jerk paste can be used with other meats, such as lamb.

Lynn Cole

# rum steaks

preparation time 10 minutes (plus marinating time) ✿ cooking time 10 minutes

4 cloves garlic, crushed
1 teaspoon salt
1/2 teaspoon freshly ground black pepper
1 tablespoon dry red wine
4 thin rump steaks (800g)
50g butter
2 medium brown onions (300g),
   sliced thinly
2 tablespoons dark rum
1 tablespoon whole black peppercorns
1/2 cup (125ml) single cream

1 Combine garlic, salt, pepper and wine in small bowl. Arrange steaks on a plate, spread wine mixture over top, cover; refrigerate at least 1 hour.

2 Melt butter in medium heavy-based frying pan; sear steaks over high heat, in batches, not more than 1 minute each side. Set steaks aside in warm place.

3 Reduce heat to medium, add onion to same pan; cook until onion is soft and beginning to brown.

4 Add rum and peppercorns; stir well. Reduce heat to low; add cream, stirring. Bring sauce to boiling point; remove from heat.

5 Pour sauce over steaks to serve.

SERVES 4

Jamaica Tourist Board

# sausages and beans

1¼ cups (250g) dried haricot beans
50g butter
500g pork sausages
2 medium brown onions (300g),
   chopped coarsely
3 cloves garlic, crushed
2 tablespoons finely chopped
   fresh flat–leaf parsley
1 tablespoon finely chopped
   fresh sage leaves
1 teaspoon fresh thyme
salt, to taste
½ teaspoon freshly ground black pepper
½ cup (125ml) dry white wine
400g tin tomatoes, chopped

1 Soak haricot beans overnight in large bowl of cold water.

2 Drain beans, place in large suacepan; cover with cold water. Bring to a boil; simmer, covered, 1 hour or until beans are tender. Drain; set aside.

3 Melt butter in large heavy-based frying pan. Prick sausages with a fork; cook sausages, turning, 8 minutes or until browned all over and cooked through. Set aside.

4 Add onion and garlic to same pan; cook until onion is golden brown and soft.

5 Drain excess fat from pan, add cooked sausages, herbs, salt and pepper; stir well. Return pan to heat, add beans, wine and undrained tomatoes; simmer, uncovered, stirring, until sausages and beans are heated through and liquid has thickened. Serve topped with a sprig of thyme, if desired.

SERVES 4

tips  If you prefer, use two 400g cans haricot beans, drained and rinsed, and omit steps 1 and 2.

This recipe can be made with beef sausages instead of pork. If using beef sausages, substitute fresh marjoram for the sage.

# caribbean
# pork roast

preparation time 15 minutes (plus marinating time)
cooking time 2 hours 30 minutes

2kg leg of pork, with rind
12 cloves
2 tablespoons dark rum
1 tablespoon dark brown sugar
2 teaspoons finely grated lime rind
1/3 cup (80ml) lime juice
1/2 teaspoon ground nutmeg
1/2 teaspoon ground coriander
1/2 teaspoon salt
1 tablespoon olive oil
1 cup (250ml) orange juice
1 tablespoon soy sauce

1  Score pork rind, right through to flesh. Press cloves deeply into score marks. Place pork in baking dish.

2  Combine rum, sugar, rind, lime juice, spices, salt and oil in small bowl. Pour rum mixture over pork, directing mixture into score marks, cover; refrigerate 3 hours, occasionally spooning marinade into score marks.

3  Preheat oven to moderate.

4  Roast pork, uncovered, in moderate oven 2 hours, basting occasionally.

5  Increase oven temperature to moderately hot; roast pork, uncovered, in moderately hot oven further 20 minutes. This will make the skin (crackling) crisper. Remove pork from dish; set aside in warm place.

6  Skim off any excess fat from pan juices in baking dish; discard fat. Add orange juice; mix well with pan juices. Pour juice mixture into small saucepan, add soy sauce, bring to a boil; boil, uncovered, until sauce has reduced by a third.

7  Remove crackling and carve pork; discard cloves. Serve pork with sauce and crackling, and a selection of vegetables, if desired.

SERVES 6

# creole pork

preparation time 30 minutes ✿ cooking time 1 hour 20 minutes

**2 medium aubergines (600g)**
**coarse cooking salt**
**2 tablespoons olive oil**
**1kg pork fillet, cut into 2cm cubes**
**1 large brown onion (200g), sliced finely**
**2 cloves garlic, crushed**
**400g tin tomatoes, drained, chopped**
**1 green chilli, chopped finely**
**1/2 teaspoon salt**
**1/2 teaspoon freshly ground black pepper**
**1/2 cup (125ml) chicken stock**

1. Slice aubergines into 1cm-thick rounds. Place rounds on paper towel, sprinkle lightly with cooking salt, then top with paper towel; smooth paper towel over rounds. Stand 20 minutes; discard paper towel. Rinse aubergine under cold water, pat dry with paper towel; chop aubergine slices into 1cm cubes.
2. Heat oil in large heavy-base saucepan; cook pork, in batches, until brown all over. Set aside.
3. Add onion, garlic and aubergine to same pan; cook 10 minutes or until onion is beginning to brown and aubergine has absorbed most of the oil.
4. Add pork, tomato, chilli, salt, black pepper and stock; simmer, covered, stirring occasionally, 1 hour.
5. Serve with plain boiled rice and a crunchy mixed-leaf salad, if desired.

SERVES 4

# st martin's island stew

preparation time 30 minutes ✿ cooking time 1 hour 30 minutes

*The island of St Martin is part of the Dutch Antilles, and this recipe reflects the Dutch influence there,*
*with the use of beer as a cooking liquid and gherkins, stuffed olives and capers for flavouring.*

50g butter
1kg trimmed diced lamb
2 medium brown onions (300g),
   chopped coarsely
4 cloves garlic, sliced
1 trimmed stick celery (75g),
   chopped coarsely
1 tablespoon grated fresh ginger root
2 fresh red chillies, seeded,
   chopped finely
1 medium yellow capsicum (200g),
   cut into 1cm squares
400g tin tomatoes, drained, chopped
1 teaspoon finely grated lime rind
2 tablespoons lime juice
1 teaspoon ground cumin
1 teaspoon ground allspice
2 cups (500ml) beer, approximately
100g gherkins, drained
2 tablespoons drained capers, rinsed
100g green pimiento-stuffed olives

1 Melt butter in large saucepan; cook lamb, in batches, until browned all over. Set aside.

2 Add onion, garlic, celery, ginger, chilli and capsicum to same pan; cook until onion is soft.

3 Add lamb, tomato, rind, juice, spices and enough beer to cover ingredients; simmer gently, covered, 1 hour or until lamb is cooked through.

4 Add gherkins, capers and olives; simmer, uncovered, 15 minutes.

SERVES 4

*Lynn Cole*

There are so many different fish available in the Caribbean that a style of cooking has been developed that works with most varieties. In these recipes we have suggested a type of fish to use, but you should not feel inhibited about swapping salmon for cod, or snapper for plaice. Each variety of fish brings a different result when matched with the tropical ingredients.

# seared tuna steaks with tropical salsa

preparation time 20 minutes (plus marinating time) ✿ cooking time 18 minutes (plus standing time)

6 tuna steaks (900g)
2 tablespoons lime juice
2 tablespoons olive oil
1 small mango (300g), chopped finely
1/2 small papaya (325g), chopped finely
1 small fresh red chilli, chopped finely
1 teaspoon finely grated lime rind
2 tablespoons lime juice, extra
1 tablespoon olive oil, extra
2 tablespoons coarsely chopped
   fresh coriander leaves

1 Place fish in shallow glass or ceramic dish; drizzle with juice and oil. Cover; refrigerate 2 hours, turning fish once during marinating time.

2 Combine mango, papaya, chilli, rind, extra juice, extra oil and coriander in large bowl. Cover; refrigerate salsa about 1 hour.

3 Heat large frying pan until very hot; cook fish, in batches, 3 minutes each side. Transfer to a plate, cover loosely with foil; stand 5 minutes.

4 Serve fish with tropical salsa.

SERVES 6

**serving suggestion** Serve with plain boiled rice.

Jamaica Tourist Board

# saltfish and ackee

preparation time 20 minutes (plus soaking time) ✿ cooking time 40 minutes

*This recipe is a Jamaican classic. Ackee is a fruit that was originally imported into the Caribbean from Africa. It is available only in tins in other parts of the world. Ackee flesh is pale yellow, not very sweet, and has a texture rather like that of lychee. If you can't find canned ackee, substitute yellow capsicums, blanched in boiling water until soft then cut into 2cm squares.*

500g salt cod
60g butter
1 large brown onion (200g),
    chopped coarsely
2 cloves garlic, crushed
2 small tomatoes (260g),
    chopped coarsely
1 green chilli, seeded, chopped finely
1/2 cup (125ml) water
1 teaspoon fresh thyme
1/2 teaspoon ground allspice
2 tablespoons finely chopped
    spring onions
freshly ground black pepper, to taste
2 x 350g cans ackee, drained

1　Soak fish overnight in large bowl of cold water.

2　Drain fish, rinse under cold water; place in large saucepan, cover with cold water. Bring to a boil, reduce heat; simmer, uncovered, 20 minutes, drain. Remove and discard skin and bones; flake flesh. Set aside.

3　Melt butter in large heavy-based saucepan. Add brown onion and garlic; cook until onion is soft. Add tomato and chilli, reduce heat; simmer gently, uncovered, stirring occasionally, 5 minutes.

4　Add fish, the water, thyme, allspice, spring onion and black pepper; stir well. Bring to a boil; simmer, uncovered, 2 minutes.

5　Add ackee; stir gently, taking care not to break up the fruit too much. Simmer until heated through.

SERVES 4

**serving suggestion**  Serve with boiled rice or, for an extra Caribbean touch, boiled or roasted green bananas.

# capsicum snapper

2 tablespoons plain flour
1/2 teaspoon salt
1/4 teaspoon freshly ground black pepper
4 snapper fillets (700g)
50g butter
1 large brown onion (200g), sliced finely
2 cloves garlic, crushed
2 medium red capsicums (400g), cut into 1cm strips
1/2 cup (125ml) dry white wine
5 medium tomatoes (1kg), peeled, seeded, chopped finely
4 spring onions, chopped finely

1  Combine flour, salt and black pepper in medium shallow dish. Toss fish in seasoned flour, shake off excess.

2  Melt butter in large frying pan; cook fish, in batches, 2 minutes each side or until golden brown. Set aside.

3  Add brown onion, garlic and capsicum to same pan; cook until onion is soft.

4  Add wine and tomato, bring to a boil; return fish to pan, covering it with vegetables and juices. Cover; simmer 10 minutes.

5  Serve sprinkled with spring onion.

SERVES 4

# cod mangolade

2 tablespoons plain flour
$1/2$ teaspoon salt
$1/2$ teaspoon freshly ground black pepper
4 cod steaks (700g)
$1/4$ cup (80g) mango chutney
$1/4$ cup (80g) thick-cut marmalade
2 teaspoons coarse-grain mustard
2 teaspoons bottled grated horseradish
50g butter
$1/2$ cup (125ml) mango puree
1 tablespoon finely chopped
   fresh mint leaves
$1/2$ teaspoon ground nutmeg

1 Combine flour, salt and pepper on a plate. Toss fish in seasoned flour, shake off excess.

2 Combine chutney, marmalade, mustard and horseradish in medium bowl, cover; refrigerate.

3 Melt butter in large heavy-based frying pan; cook fish about 5 minutes on each side. Set aside; keep warm.

4 Add mango puree, mint and nutmeg to same pan, stir into pan juices; bring to a boil. Return fish to pan, cover; cook until heated through.

5 Serve fish with mango and mint puree, accompanied by chilled chutney mixture (mangolade).

SERVES 4

tip If you prefer, use halibut or turbot instead of cod.

serving suggestion This dish can be served with mashed potato, spiced with $1/2$ teaspoon Angostura bitters, and lime wedges.

# bream with tomato coriander salsa

preparation time 25 minutes ✿ cooking time 30 minutes

4 large tomatoes (1kg), peeled,
   seeded, chopped finely
1 green chilli, chopped finely
1 small red onion (100g), chopped finely
2 tablespoons lime juice
3 tablespoons finely chopped
   fresh coriander leaves
salt, to taste
pepper, to taste
4 medium potatoes (800g), peeled,
   cut into even-sized pieces
100g butter
4 bream fillets (about 750g)
1 teaspoon sweet paprika

1 Combine tomato, chilli, onion, juice, coriander, salt and pepper in large bowl; set aside.

2 Place potato in large saucepan of cold water with 1 teaspoon salt. Bring to a boil, reduce heat; simmer, uncovered, 15-20 minutes or until potato is tender.

3 Meanwhile, melt half of the butter in grill pan. Add fish; turn so that fillets are coated in melted butter on both sides. Sprinkle fish with a little extra salt and pepper; cook, turning once, 6 minutes or until lightly browned all over and cooked through.

4 Drain potatoes; mash with remaining butter and paprika. Add a little milk if you prefer a moister mash.

5 Serve each fillet on a bed of mashed potato with tomato coriander salsa.

SERVES 4

# barbecued prawns

preparation time 20 minutes (plus marinating time)
cooking time 5 minutes

*Soak wooden barbecue skewers in cold water for at least 1 hour before using, to prevent them scorching.*

2 teaspoons finely grated lime rind
1/3 cup (80ml) lime juice
1 green chilli, chopped finely
2 tablespoons grated fresh ginger root
3 cloves garlic, crushed
2 teaspoons light brown sugar
1 teaspoon ground allspice
1 tablespoon sweet chilli sauce
1/3 cup (80ml) olive oil
16 uncooked jumbo prawns (650g)

1   Combine rind, juice, chilli pepper, ginger, garlic, sugar, allspice, sauce and oil in large bowl. Add prawns, cover; refrigerate 1 hour, turning prawns at least once during marinating time.

2   Thread prawns onto four wooden barbecue skewers.

3   Cook prawns on barbecue, brushing occasionally with the marinade and turning at least once, about 5 minutes or until prawns are changed in colour and firm-fleshed.

SERVES 4

**tip**   Fresh or frozen prawns can be used in this recipe.

# trout with mango and ginger

preparation time 20 minutes ✿ cooking time 45 minutes

*Although most Caribbean fish recipes use saltwater fish, some freshwater fish dishes are also popular. The vivid colour and wonderful taste of the mango, plus the delicate flavour of tarragon, make this a memorable dish.*

2 tablespoons plain flour

1/2 teaspoon salt

1/2 teaspoon freshly ground black pepper

4 small trout (about 1.5kg),
   cleaned and scaled

2 medium mangoes (860g), seeded,
   chopped coarsely

3 cloves garlic, crushed

1 tablespoon finely chopped
   fresh tarragon

1 medium brown onion (150g),
   chopped finely

2 medium tomatoes (380g),
   chopped finely

2 tablespoons grated fresh ginger root

1 teaspoon light brown sugar

1 cup (250ml) fish stock

50g butter

2 spring onions, cut into long strips

1 Combine flour, salt and pepper on a plate. Toss fish in seasoned flour, shake off excess.

2 Blend or process mango, garlic, tarragon, brown onion, tomato, ginger, sugar and stock until smooth; set aside.

3 Melt butter in large heavy-based frying pan; cook fish, in batches, occasionally pressing fish into pan with flat side of an egg-lifter, 6 minutes each side or until well browned all over. Set aside in warm place.

4 Add blended sauce to same pan, stir into pan juices. Bring to a boil; simmer, uncovered, 2 minutes, then return fish to pan. Spoon sauce over fish, cover; simmer gently 15 minutes, turning fish once.

5 Serve fish topped with sauce and spring onion.

SERVES 4

tip If you prefer, use 2 teaspoons dried tarragon in place of the fresh tarragon.

# trinidad fish bake

preparation time 10 minutes (plus marinating time) ❀ cooking time 30 minutes

1 cup (280g) plain yogurt
1 tablespoon curry powder
1 tablespoon desiccated coconut
2 shallots, chopped finely
2 cloves garlic, crushed
1 tablespoon olive oil
$1/2$ teaspoon salt
$1/2$ teaspoon freshly ground black pepper
3 teaspoons finely grated lime rind
$1/2$ cup (125ml) lime juice
4 halibut steaks (700g)

1 Preheat oven to moderate.

2 Combine yogurt, curry powder, coconut, shallot, garlic, oil, salt, pepper, rind and juice in shallow baking dish. Add fish, spooning yogurt mixture over fish to coat. Cover; refrigerate at least 1 hour.

3 Bake fish, uncovered, in moderate oven 30 minutes, occasionally basting fish with marinade.

4 Serve with lime wedges, if desired.

SERVES 4

tip If you prefer, use cod steaks instead of halibut.

Jamaica Tourist Board

# baked salmon steaks

2 tablespoons fresh lime juice
2 cloves garlic, crushed
2 teaspoons sweet chilli sauce
2 tablespoons olive oil
4 salmon steaks (700g)
1 lime, cut into eight thin slices

1  Preheat oven to moderate.

2  Combine juice, garlic, sauce and oil in small bowl; whisk until blended.

3  Lightly oil large piece of foil, place on oven tray. Place fish on foil, turn up edges of foil; pour lime juice mixture over fish.

4  Place two slices of lime on each fish steak. Place another sheet of foil over top; fold foil edges to seal tightly.

5  Bake fish in moderate oven 10 minutes; stand 5 minutes before opening foil and serving.

SERVES 4

**serving suggestion**  Serve with thin barbecued slices of red sweet potato and a crispy green salad.

# crab gumbo

preparation time 20 minutes ✿ cooking time 20 minutes

400g white cabbage, chopped coarsely
400g spinach leaves, stems removed
200g watercress
1 cup fresh flat-leaf parsley leaves
50g butter
2 medium brown onions (300g),
    chopped finely
2 medium tomatoes (380g),
    chopped coarsely
1 fresh red chilli, chopped finely
1 teaspoon fresh thyme leaves
1 teaspoon finely chopped
    fresh marjoram
1 teaspoon ground allspice
$1/2$ teaspoon salt
$1/2$ teaspoon freshly ground
    black pepper
400g fresh crab meat
100g radishes, sliced thinly

1  Place cabbage, spinach, watercress and parsley in large saucepan with just enough water to cover. Bring to a boil; simmer, uncovered, 1 minute. Drain vegetables; reserve liquid. Chop vegetables finely.

2  Melt butter in large heavy-based saucepan; cook onion, stirring, until lightly browned. Add chopped vegetables, tomato, chilli, thyme, marjoram, allspice, salt and black pepper; stir well. Add 1 cup of the reserved vegetable liquid, bring to a boil; simmer, uncovered, 5 minutes or until liquid has almost evaporated.

3  Add crab meat and radish; stir until heated through.

4  Serve crab gumbo with boiled rice, if desired.

SERVES 4

tip  If you prefer, use $1/2$ teaspoon dried thyme and $1/2$ teaspoon dried marjoram in place of fresh thyme and fresh marjoram. Frozen or tinned crab meat can be used instead of fresh crab meat.

Jamaica Tourist Board

*In modern cookery, the word "salsa" refers to wonderfully tangy combinations of sweet and savoury fruit and vegetables that accompany the main meal. Other traditional accompaniments to Caribbean cooking include potatoes – sweet or otherwise – rice, okra, aubergine and a variety of legumes such as pigeon peas, black-eyed beans, haricot beans and red kidney beans. We have used tinned beans in these recipes but, if you prefer, you can substitute dried beans. Soak dried beans overnight in cold water, rinse them, then simmer in boiling salted water until they are tender.*

# hoppin' john

preparation time 15 minutes ✿ cooking time 35 minutes

*This dish is traditionally eaten on New Year's Day, when it is said to bring good luck for the year ahead.*

3 cups (750ml) chicken stock
1 large tomato (250g), chopped coarsely
1/3 cup finely chopped spring onions
1 green chilli, seeded, chopped finely
2 teaspoons fresh thyme leaves
1 bay leaf
1/2 teaspoon saffron threads
12 whole black peppercorns
1 1/4 cups (250g) white long-grain rice
4 rashers thick-cut back bacon,
   cut into large pieces
450g tin black-eyed beans, drained
salt, to taste

1 Bring stock to a boil in large saucepan, add tomato, onion, chilli, thyme, bay leaf, saffron and peppercorns; boil, uncovered, 2 minutes. Add rice; simmer, uncovered, stirring occasionally, 15 minutes. If necessary, add a little water to prevent rice from drying out.

2 Meanwhile, cook bacon in medium non-stick frying pan until cooked through, but not crisp.

3 Stir bacon and beans into rice mixture; simmer, uncovered, stirring occasionally, 10 minutes or until rice is cooked and liquid is absorbed.

4 Discard bay leaf; add salt before serving.

SERVES 4

Jamaica Tourist Board

# mango salsa

1 medium mango (430g), seeded,
  chopped finely
1 medium red onion (170g),
  chopped finely
1 medium red capsicum (200g),
  chopped finely
1 tablespoon finely chopped
  fresh marjoram
1/2 teaspoon ground ginger
1 tablespoon olive oil

1 Combine ingredients in medium bowl, cover; refrigerate until cold.

2 Serve salsa with any barbecued dish.

SERVES 4

# sweet potato stir

2 small red sweet potatoes (500g),
  cut into 2cm pieces
1 teaspoon salt
2 tablespoons olive oil
1 large brown onion (200g),
  chopped coarsely
2 cloves garlic, sliced finely
1 teaspoon ground cumin
450g tin red kidney beans, drained
1 teaspoon finely grated lime rind
2 tablespoons lime juice
2 tablespoons finely chopped fresh
  coriander leaves

1 Place potato and salt in large saucepan of cold water. Bring to a boil,
  reduce heat; simmer, uncovered, until potato is just tender, drain.
  Do not overcook, or potato will become mushy when fried.

2 Heat oil in large frying pan, add potato; cook 5 minutes or until potato
  is beginning to brown. Add onion and garlic; cook, using an egg-lifter to
  turn potato without breaking, until onion is beginning to brown.

3 Add cumin, beans, rind and juice; cook until beans are heated through.

4 Stir coriander through mixture just before serving.

SERVES 4

# hot barbecue salsa

preparation time 15 minutes  ✿  cooking time 15 minutes

1 tablespoon olive oil
1 medium brown onion (150g),
    chopped coarsely
2 cloves garlic, crushed
2 green chillies, seeded, chopped finely
400g tin tomatoes, drained,
    seeded, chopped
1 tablespoon finely chopped fresh
    flat-leaf parsley
1 teaspoon hot paprika
1/2 teaspoon salt
1/2 teaspoon freshly ground black pepper

1 Heat oil in medium saucepan; cook onion and garlic until onion is soft.

2 Add remaining ingredients to pan; simmer, uncovered, 10 minutes.

3 Serve warm salsa with barbecued beef, lamb or chicken, if desired.

SERVES 4

# sweet and sour salad

preparation time 15 minutes

2 medium oranges (480g)
2 tablespoons plain yogurt
2 tablespoons lime juice
300g shredded white cabbage
1 medium apple (150g), grated coarsely
1 Lebanese cucumber (130g),
    sliced finely
2 medium tomatoes (380g),
    chopped coarsely

1 Peel and thinly slice oranges; cut slices into quarters.

2 Combine yogurt and juice in small bowl or jug; stir until smooth.

3 Combine orange with remaining ingredients in large bowl; drizzle with yogurt mixture, toss to combine.

SERVES 6

# lentil salsa

preparation time 15 minutes  ✿  cooking time 35 minutes

1/2 cup (100g) green lentils
1 cup (250ml) cold water
2 tablespoons finely chopped
    fresh coriander leaves
2 large tomatoes (500g), peeled,
    seeded, cut into 1cm pieces
1/2 medium red onion (85g),
    chopped finely
1 fresh red chilli, seeded, chopped finely
2 tablespoons lime juice
2 tablespoons olive oil
salt, to taste
freshly ground black pepper, to taste

1 Rinse lentils under cold water. Place in medium saucepan with the water, bring to a boil. Cover, reduce heat; simmer 30 minutes or until lentils are just tender.

2 Rinse lentils under cold water; drain. Place lentils in medium bowl, add remaining ingredients; stir well. Cover; refrigerate until cold.

3 Serve salsa with fish or chicken, if desired.

SERVES 4

*clockwise from top left: lentil salsa,*
*sweet and sour salad, hot barbecue salsa*

# barbados cou-cou

preparation time 5 minutes ✿ cooking time 35 minutes

*Traditional cou-cou is made with cornmeal. We have substituted the more readily available polenta, made from ground maize, which gives the same result.*

400g okra, trimmed, sliced thickly
1 teaspoon salt
3 cups (750ml) cold water
3/4 cup (180ml) coconut milk
1 1/2 cups (250g) polenta
30g butter
1/2 teaspoon freshly ground
   black pepper

1 Place okra in large saucepan with salt and the water. Bring to a boil, reduce heat; simmer, uncovered, about 10 minutes. Drain okra; reserve cooking liquid.

2 Pour coconut milk and about 1/2 cup (125ml) of the reserved cooking liquid into large saucepan; bring to a boil. Add okra, then gradually add polenta, beating vigorously. If necessary, add more reserved cooking liquid to keep the polenta moist but not runny; cook, uncovered, stirring constantly so that polenta doesn't stick to bottom of pan, 5 minutes. Cover; cook 10 minutes, stirring occasionally.

3 To serve, spread cou-cou with butter; sprinkle with pepper.

SERVES 4

# green papaya salsa

preparation time 20 minutes

2 tablespoons lime juice
2 teaspoons dark brown sugar
1 teaspoon finely grated lime rind
1 medium green papaya (1kg),
   seeded, chopped finely
2 tablespoons finely chopped
   fresh coriander leaves
1 fresh red chilli, seeded, chopped finely
1 medium red onion (170g),
   chopped finely
1 tablespoon olive oil

1 Place juice in large bowl, add sugar; stir until sugar is dissolved. Add remaining ingredients; stir well. Cover; refrigerate until cold.

2 Serve salsa with grilled fish or barbecued chicken, if desired.

SERVES 8

*Just about any combination of tropical fruit, eaten on its own or with cream or ice-cream, makes a Caribbean dessert. We suggest a few special recipes that make original use of typical Caribbean ingredients.*

# coconut ice-cream

preparation time 20 minutes (plus freezing time) ❉ cooking time 20 minutes

3 egg yolks
2 teaspoons cornflour
½ cup (110g) caster sugar
2 cups (500ml) coconut milk
¼ cup (60ml) single cream
1 tablespoon curaçao

1 Whisk egg yolks in medium bowl. Add cornflour and sugar; whisk until mixture thickens, set aside.

2 Heat coconut milk in medium saucepan until very hot, do not boil; pour milk into egg mixture, whisk. Return mixture to same pan; cook, uncovered, stirring constantly, until mixture thickens and forms a custard.

3 Pour mixture into medium bowl; cool. Whisk cream and curaçao into cooled mixture, pour into plastic tub (an old ice-cream tub is perfect); freeze 2 hours.

4 Beat ice-cream mixture in large bowl with electric mixer until smooth but not melted. Pour ice-cream into same plastic tub; freeze 2 hours. Beat again; freeze until firm.

SERVES 4

tips As well as adding flavour, the curaçao helps prevent gritty ice crystals from forming, leaving the mixture smooth and creamy.

If you prefer, use brandy or Cointreau instead of curaçao.

Lynn Cole

# duckanoo

preparation time 20 minutes ✿ cooking time 30 minutes

*There are endless variations on this traditional recipe. Some cooks prefer to omit the flour, using only polenta, and, rather than baking, poach the duckanoo in gently boiling water about 10 minutes.*

$^1/_2$ cup (85g) polenta
$^2/_3$ cup (100g) self-raising flour
150g fresh coconut, grated finely
$^1/_2$ teaspoon vanilla essence
1 cup (250ml) milk
$^1/_3$ cup (55g) raisins
$^1/_4$ cup (50g) dark brown sugar
$^1/_2$ teaspoon grated fresh nutmeg
$^1/_2$ teaspoon ground cinnamon
2 tablespoons cold water
20g butter

1  Preheat oven to moderate.

2  Combine polenta, flour and coconut in large bowl. Gradually add blended vanilla and milk, stirring constantly, until mixture is smooth.

3  Add raisins, sugar, nutmeg and cinnamon; stir until mixed through. Add the water and melted butter; knead until mixture is even.

4  Roll mixture into golf-ball-sized portions; place balls on greased oven tray.

5  Bake duckanoo in moderate oven 30 minutes or until golden.

6  Serve duckanoo with cream or ice-cream, if desired.

**SERVES 6 (MAKES 18)**

**tip** Fresh coconut delivers the best results in this recipe, but you can substitute desiccated coconut, if you prefer.

# ginger syllabub

preparation time 20 minutes (plus refrigeration time)

1¼ cups (300ml) double cream

30g caster sugar

¼ cup (60ml) dark rum

2 globes bottled stem ginger, drained, chopped finely

1 tablespoon bottled stem-ginger syrup

½ teaspoon ground ginger

½ teaspoon grated fresh nutmeg

1 teaspoon finely grated lime rind

2 tablespoons lime juice

12 ginger biscuits

1 Beat cream and sugar in large bowl with electric mixer until mixture begins to stiffen. Gently fold through rum, stem ginger, syrup, ground ginger, nutmeg, rind and juice.

2 Pour cream mixture into four glasses; refrigerate 1½ hours.

3 Serve syllabub with ginger biscuits.

SERVES 4

# lime syrup

preparation time 10 minutes (plus refrigeration time)  ✿  cooking time 25 minutes

*This basic syrup can be used with ice-cream or fresh fruit. It goes well with coconut
ice-cream, and is delicious poured over fresh papaya or mango.*

**1 lime**
**¹/₂ cup (110g) caster sugar**
**¹/₂ cup (125ml) water**
**¹/₂ cup (125ml) lime juice**
**1 teaspoon cornflour**

1  Peel lime, avoiding the bitter white pith; cut rind into fine strips.

2  Combine sugar and the water in small saucepan; add lime rind, bring to a
boil. Simmer gently, covered, 15 minutes.

3  Add blended juice and cornflour to pan; stir well. Simmer gently,
uncovered, stirring constantly, 3 minutes or until mixture thickens
and looks transparent; cool.

4  Refrigerate syrup 1 hour before serving.

SERVES 4

# grilled mango cheeks

preparation time 15 minutes ✿ cooking time 12 minutes

**4 medium mangoes (1.7kg)**
**1 tablespoon dark brown sugar**
**2 tablespoons dark rum**

1  Peel mangoes; cut two cheeks from each mango by slicing lengthways on either side of seed.

2  Preheat oven to moderately hot.

3  Place mango cheeks, flat-side down, in grill pan; cook until mango starts to brown.

4  Transfer mango to baking dish; sprinkle sugar and rum over mango.

5  Bake mango, uncovered, in moderately hot oven 8 minutes.

6  Top mango with passionfruit pulp and serve with cream or ice-cream, if desired.

SERVES 4

**tip**  This recipe uses only the mango cheeks; use any remaining mango flesh in a salsa or salad.

*The drinks of the Caribbean are already well known around the world – there are few international cocktail bars without a favourite recipe for piña colada, daiquiri or Cuba libre. But other Caribbean favourites, such as the unusual stout punch, have remained an island secret. As with all Caribbean recipes, the key to success lies with the use of fresh ingredients where possible.*

# piña colada

preparation time 5 minutes

1 cup (250ml) coconut cream
1 cup (250ml) rum (dark or white)
1¹/2 cups (375ml) pineapple juice
1 cup cracked ice
1 lime, sliced thinly

1 Blend coconut cream, rum and juice in a blender or cocktail shaker about 30 seconds.

2 Add ice; blend or shake 30 seconds.

3 Serve in tall glasses, with a slice of lime.

SERVES 4

# cream stout punch

preparation time 5 minutes (plus refrigeration time)

*Cream stout punch is a Caribbean classic. The ingredients are certainly unusual, but it can be curiously refreshing on a tropical day.*

400g tin condensed milk
400g tin evaporated milk
1 teaspoon vanilla essence
¹/2 cup (100g) light brown sugar
¹/2 cup (125ml) white rum
600ml stout

1 Beat condensed milk, evaporated milk, vanilla, sugar and rum in large bowl with electric mixer until combined.

2 Pour milk mixture into large jug; add stout, stir well.

3 Refrigerate punch at least 1 hour. Serve in tumblers.

SERVES 4

*left to right: cream stout punch; piña colada*

Jamaica Tourist Board

# fruit daiquiri

preparation time 10 minutes

1 lime
1 cup (250ml) dark rum
1 tablespoon dark brown sugar
1/2 cup (125ml) lime juice
1/2 cup (125ml) pineapple juice
3 passionfruit
1/4 teaspoon Angostura bitters
2 cups cracked ice

1 Peel lime, avoiding bitter white pith; reserve rind.

2 Combine rum, sugar, juices, passionfruit pulp, bitters and ice in cocktail shaker; shake briefly or until combined.

3 Serve in cocktail glasses, decorated with a little reserved rind.

SERVES 4

# carib champagne

preparation time 5 minutes

1 tablespoon curaçao
2 cups (500ml) chilled champagne
1 tablespoon dark rum
1 cup (250ml) chilled
   pineapple juice

1 Combine ingredients in large jug.

2 Serve in champagne glasses.

SERVES 4

# fruit punch

preparation time 5 minutes

*This drink contains no alcohol.*

1 1/4 cups (310ml) fresh orange juice
1 1/4 cups (310ml) grapefruit juice
1 1/4 cups (310ml) pineapple juice
1 1/4 cups (310ml) ginger ale
1/2 cup (125ml) lime syrup
   (see recipe page 101)
1/4 teaspoon Angostura bitters
2 cups ice cubes
4 fresh mint leaves
1 lime, sliced thinly

1 Combine juices, ginger ale, syrup, bitters and ice in large jug.

2 Serve in tall glasses, decorated with mint and slices of lime.

SERVES 4

*left to right: carib champagne;
fruit daiquiri; fruit punch*

**ackee** a red-skinned, pear-shaped fruit originally from Africa but now grown widely in the West Indies. Fresh ackee is almost impossible to obtain outside the Caribbean, but tinned ackee can be found in specialist food shops and some supermarkets. The tinned variety has soft, fragile yellow flesh.

**allspice** also known as pimento or Jamaican pepper; available whole or ground. Tastes like a blend of cinnamon, clove and nutmeg.

**angostura aromatic bitters** Angostura is a brand name for a type of bitters. It is based on rum, infused with bitter aromatic bark, herbs and spices.

**aniseed** also called anise; the licorice-flavoured seeds of the anise plant.

**baking powder** a raising agent consisting mainly of two parts cream of tartar to one part bicarbonate of soda (baking soda).

**banana, green** an ordinary banana that has been picked before it is fully ripe. Bananas with a long journey to market are usually picked green and ripened in warm cellars at their destination. Green bananas have not undergone this ripening process; they are firmer with green, rather than yellow, skin.

**beans**

BLACK-EYED also known as black-eyed peas; small beige legumes with black circular eyes. Available dried or tinned.

HARICOT small white variety of common beans; sold dried or tinned.

RED KIDNEY pink to maroon beans with a floury texture and fairly sweet flavour; sold dried or tinned.

**bouquet garni** a combination of thyme, parsley and a bay leaf, tied together with kitchen string or placed in a muslin bag; used in soups and stews; it is usually removed before serving.

**butter** use salted or unsalted butter.

**capers** the grey-green buds of a warm-climate (usually Mediterranean) shrub, sold either dried and salted or pickled in a vinegar brine; used to enhance sauces and dressings with their piquant flavour.

ackee

**capsicum** also known as peppers or bell peppers; available in a variety of colours. Seeds and membranes should be discarded before use.

**cardamom** an expensive spice with an exotic flavour. Can be purchased in pod, seed or ground form.

**cayenne pepper** very hot spice made from dried ground pods of chillies.

**chicken**

BREAST has skin and bone intact.

BREAST FILLET breast halved, skinned and boned.

DRUMSTICK leg with skin intact.

THIGH has skin and bone intact.

**chickpeas** also called garbanzos or channa; irregularly round, sandy-coloured legumes used extensively in Caribbean, Mediterranean and Middle-Eastern cooking.

**chilli** also known as chilli pepper, chiles and hot peppers; available in many different types and sizes. Use rubber gloves when seeding and chopping fresh chilli, as they can burn your skin. Removing seeds and membranes reduces the heat level.

POWDER made from ground chilli, it can be used as a substitute for fresh chilli peppers in the proportion of 1/2 teaspoon ground chilli powder to one medium chopped fresh chilli pepper.

SAUCE we used a hot Chinese variety made of chilli peppers, salt and vinegar; use sparingly, increasing amounts to taste.

SWEET CHILLI SAUCE a comparatively mild, but spicy sauce made from red chilli peppers, sugar, garlic and vinegar.

**chives** a herb with a subtle onion flavour.

**cinnamon** a spice obtained from the dried inner bark of the cinnamon tree.

**cloves** the dried flower buds of a tropical tree; can be used whole or in ground form.

**coconut**

CREAM available in tins and cartons; as a rule, the proportions are two parts coconut to one part water.

DESICCATED unsweetened, concentrated, dried, shredded coconut flesh.

MILK pure, unsweetened coconut milk available in tins and cartons.

WHOLE FRESH choose a coconut that is heavy for its size; shake to make certain it contains liquid. This liquid should not be confused with coconut milk.

**coriander** also known as cilantro or Chinese parsley; a bright-green leafy herb with a pungent flavour. Often stirred into a dish just before serving for maximum impact.

**cornflour** a thickening agent that is also known as cornstarch.

**crab meat** flesh of fresh crabs. Use tinned if fresh is unavailable.

**curaçao** an orange-flavoured liqueur.

**cumin** a warm, pungent spice used mainly in savoury dishes; available as seeds or in ground form.

**curry powder** a mixture in powdered form of coriander, chilli peppers, cumin, fennel, cinnamon, fenugreek and turmeric in varying proportions.

**flour**

WHITE PLAIN an all-purpose flour, made from wheat.

WHITE SELF-RAISING substitute plain (all-purpose) flour and baking powder in the proportion of 1 cup plain flour to 2 teaspoons baking powder.

**garam masala** a spice mixture consisting of varying combinations of cardamom, cinnamon, cloves, cumin, coriander and fennel roasted and ground together.

**gherkin** also known as a cornichon; a young, dark-green cucumber grown especially for pickling.

**ginger root**

FRESH also known as green ginger; the thick gnarled root of a tropical plant. Peel away the outside skin and it is ready to grate, chop or slice as required.

GROUND also called powdered ginger; no substitute for fresh ginger root.

STEM GINGER ginger root that is preserved and bottled in syrup.

**green peppercorns** soft, unripe berries of the pepper plant usually sold in brine.

**halibut** a large, flat, seawater fish.

**horseradish cream** a creamy prepared paste of grated horseradish, vinegar, oil and sugar usually served as a condiment.

**jerk** originally the name given to dried beef or venison (called jerky by sailors). Jerking was the process used before the invention of refrigeration to preserve meat on long voyages. The jerked meat was unappetising, and cooks added strong flavours to disguise this. "Jerk" has now come to mean the fiery paste used to marinate the meat rather than the meat itself.

**lamb**

LOIN CHOP cut from the back; contains part of the backbone.

TRIMMED DICED LAMB cubed lean meat.

LEG cut from the hindquarter.

**leek** a large member of the onion family with a less pungent flavour than onion.

**lentils** a variety of dried legume, named after and identified by their colour.

**lime rind** grated skin of fresh lime.

**mace** a spice made from the outer covering of nutmeg.

**mangetout** also known as snow peas or sugar peas. Their small flat pods have tiny, barely formed peas inside; they are eaten whole, pod and all. They need to be topped and tailed, and the older ones need stringing. They require only a short cooking time, either by stir-frying or blanching.

**mango** a round fruit about the size of a large pear, with green skin turning orange-yellow when ripe; the slightly sharp flavour makes the mango a perfect ingredient for salsas and sauces. Can be eaten raw on its own or as part of

green bananas; mangoes

fruit salad; if fresh mangoes are not available, use tinned.

**CHUTNEY** a mild, sweet chutney made from mangoes and spices.

**PUREE** fresh mango flesh chopped and then blended or processed until smooth; also available frozen or in tins.

**marmalade** a jam or preserve, usually based on citrus fruit.

**milk** we used full-cream homogenised milk unless otherwise specified.

**CONDENSED** a canned milk product consisting of milk with more than half the water content removed and sugar added to the milk that remains.

**EVAPORATED** unsweetened canned milk from which water has been extracted by evaporation.

**mushrooms, button** small, white cultivated mushrooms with a delicate, subtle flavour.

**mussels** must be tightly closed when bought, indicating they are alive. Before cooking, scrub the shells with a strong brush and remove the "beards". Discard any shells that do not open after cooking.

**mustard**

**FRENCH** a smooth, mild mustard with a sweet-sour taste.

**COARSE-GRAIN** flavoursome, coarse-grained, fairly hot mustard containing white wine.

**nutmeg** the dried nut of an evergreen tree; it is available in ground form or you can grate your own with a fine grater.

**oil**

**OLIVE** made from the pressing of tree-ripened olives. Extra virgin and virgin olive oil are the highest quality, obtained from the first pressings of the olives.

**VEGETABLE** any of a number of oils from plants rather than animal fats.

**okra** also known as gumbo or lady's fingers; a green, ridged, oblong pod with a furry skin. Native to Africa, this vegetable is used in Caribbean, Indian, Mediterranean, Middle-Eastern and southern-American cooking; it is used to thicken stews. Rinse and cut off capped end close to stalk.

**onion**

**BROWN AND WHITE** most common varieties; interchangeable. Strong in flavour, used in soups, casseroles and stock.

**RED** also known as Spanish onion; sweet-flavoured, large, purple-red onion that is particularly good eaten raw in salads.

**SPRING** also known as green onion or scallion; an immature onion, with long green leaves and tiny bulb.

**paprika** ground dried red pepper, available sweet or hot.

**papaya** also known as pawpaw or papaw; large, pear-shaped red-orange tropical fruit. Sometimes used unripe (green) in cooking.

**pine nuts** also known as pignoli; small, cream-coloured kernels obtained from the cones of different varieties of pine trees.

**plantain** the banana-like fruit of a tropical plant that is usually sold green, and will ripen at room temperature to yellow, then brown and finally to black. Plantain is only edible when cooked, usually by roasting or frying. Substitute green banana if plantain is not available.

**polenta** a flour-like cereal made of ground corn (maize); similar to cornmeal but finer and lighter in colour; also the name of the dish made from it.

**pork**

**LEG** the hind leg; lean and tender, good for roasting.

**FILLET** boneless cut from the hindquarters.

**LOIN CHOP** from the hind loin.

**pumpkin** also called squash; a member of the gourd family. Various types can be substituted for one another.

**rice**

**LONG-GRAIN** elongated grain; grains remain firm and separate when cooked.

**MEDIUM-GRAIN** fatter and usually stickier than, but interchangeable with, long-grain rice.

**SHORT-GRAIN** fat, almost round grain with a high starch content; tends to clump together when cooked.

**WHITE** hulled and polished, can be short- or long-grain.

**rind** zest.

**rum** liquor made from fermented sugarcane; dark and light varieties are available.

**DARK** we prefer to use an underproof rum (not overproof) for a more subtle flavour.

**WHITE** we use Bacardi rum, which is colourless.

**saffron** the stigma of a member of the crocus family; available in strands or ground form. Saffron imparts a yellow-orange colour to food once infused. Quality varies greatly, with the best being the most expensive spice in the world. Should be stored in the freezer.

**salmon** red-pink, firm-fleshed freshwater fish with a moist delicate flavour.

**salt cod** known as baccala in Spain and Portugal, and morue in France; cod dried and preserved in salt.

This method was used in the days before refrigeration to preserve fish on long sea voyages; salt cod is now regarded as a delicacy. If unobtainable, it is possible to substitute smoked fish such as smoked cod or haddock but the flavour is not the same.

**shallots** also called French shallots, golden shallots or eschalots; small, elongated, brown-skinned members of the onion family.

**snapper** small, firm-fleshed fish sold whole; varieties include red, pink and yellowtail snapper.

**soy sauce** made from fermented soy beans. Several variations are available, among them salt-reduced, light, sweet and salty.

**spinach** delicate green leaves on thin stems; good eaten raw or steamed.

**stock** 1 cup (250ml) stock equals 1 cup (250ml) water plus one crumbled stock cube (or 1 teaspoon stock powder), or make fresh stock.

**sugar** we used coarse, granulated table sugar, also known as crystal sugar, unless otherwise specified.

**CASTER** also known as superfine or finely granulated table sugar.

**DARK BROWN** an extremely soft, fine-grained sugar retaining the deep flavour and colour of molasses.

**LIGHT BROWN** another soft, fine-grained sugar with cane molasses added.

**sweet potato** fleshy root vegetable; available with red or white flesh.

**tomato**

**PASTE** triple-concentrated tomato puree used to flavour soups, stews, sauces and casseroles.

**TINNED** whole peeled tomatoes in natural juices.

**trout** freshwater fish with cream-pink flesh; usually cooked whole.

**yogurt** an unflavoured, full-fat cow milk yogurt has been used in these recipes unless stated otherwise.

**watercress** a vegetable with small, crisp, deep-green, rounded leaves, having a slightly bitter, peppery flavour.

**worcestershire sauce** a thin, dark-brown, spicy sauce used as seasoning for meat and gravies, and as a condiment.

salt cod

# INDEX

# CONVERSION CHART

## MEASURES

One Australian metric measuring cup holds approximately 250ml; one Australian metric tablespoon holds 20ml; one Australian metric teaspoon holds 5ml.

The difference between one country's measuring cups and another's is within a two- or three-teaspoon variance, and will not affect your cooking results. North America, New Zealand and the United Kingdom use a 15ml tablespoon.

All cup and spoon measurements are level. The most accurate way of measuring dry ingredients is to weigh them. When measuring liquids, use a clear glass or plastic jug with the metric markings.

We use large eggs with an average weight of 60g.

## DRY MEASURES

| METRIC | IMPERIAL |
|---|---|
| 15g | ½oz |
| 30g | 1oz |
| 60g | 2oz |
| 90g | 3oz |
| 125g | 4oz (¼lb) |
| 155g | 5oz |
| 185g | 6oz |
| 220g | 7oz |
| 250g | 8oz (½lb) |
| 280g | 9oz |
| 315g | 10oz |
| 345g | 11oz |
| 375g | 12oz (¾lb) |
| 410g | 13oz |
| 440g | 14oz |
| 470g | 15oz |
| 500g | 16oz (1lb) |
| 750g | 24oz (1½lb) |
| 1kg | 32oz (2lb) |

## LIQUID MEASURES

| METRIC | IMPERIAL |
|---|---|
| 30ml | 1 fluid oz |
| 60ml | 2 fluid oz |
| 100ml | 3 fluid oz |
| 125ml | 4 fluid oz |
| 150ml | 5 fluid oz (¼ pint/1 gill) |
| 190ml | 6 fluid oz |
| 250ml | 8 fluid oz |
| 300ml | 10 fluid oz (½ pint) |
| 500ml | 16 fluid oz |
| 600ml | 20 fluid oz (1 pint) |
| 1000ml (1 litre) | 1¾ pints |

## LENGTH MEASURES

| METRIC | IMPERIAL |
|---|---|
| 3mm | ⅛in |
| 6mm | ¼in |
| 1cm | ½in |
| 2cm | ¾in |
| 2.5cm | 1in |
| 5cm | 2in |
| 6cm | 2½in |
| 8cm | 3in |
| 10cm | 4in |
| 13cm | 5in |
| 15cm | 6in |
| 18cm | 7in |
| 20cm | 8in |
| 23cm | 9in |
| 25cm | 10in |
| 28cm | 11in |
| 30cm | 12in (1ft) |

## OVEN TEMPERATURES

These oven temperatures are only a guide for conventional ovens. For fan-forced ovens, check the manufacturer's manual.

| | °C (CELSIUS) | °F (FAHRENHEIT) | GAS MARK |
|---|---|---|---|
| Very slow | 120 | 250 | ½ |
| Slow | 150 | 275-300 | 1-2 |
| Moderately slow | 170 | 325 | 3 |
| Moderate | 180 | 350-375 | 4-5 |
| Moderately hot | 200 | 400 | 6 |
| Hot | 220 | 425-450 | 7-8 |
| Very hot | 240 | 475 | 9 |

# ARE YOU MISSING SOME OF THE WORLD'S FAVOURITE COOKBOOKS?

The Australian Women's Weekly Cookbooks are available from bookshops, cookshops, supermarkets and other stores all over the world. You can also buy direct from the publisher, using the order form below.

| TITLE | RRP | QTY | TITLE | RRP | QTY |
|---|---|---|---|---|---|
| Asian Meals in Minutes | £6.99 | | Great Lamb Cookbook | £6.99 | |
| Babies & Toddlers Good Food | £6.99 | | Greek Cooking Class | £6.99 | |
| Barbecue Meals In Minutes | £6.99 | | Healthy Heart Cookbook | £6.99 | |
| Basic Cooking Class | £6.99 | | Indian Cooking Class | £6.99 | |
| Beginners Cooking Class | £6.99 | | Japanese Cooking Class | £6.99 | |
| Beginners Simple Meals | £6.99 | | Kids' Birthday Cakes | £6.99 | |
| Beginners Thai | £6.99 | | Kids Cooking | £6.99 | |
| Best Food | £6.99 | | Lean Food | £6.99 | |
| Best Food Desserts | £6.99 | | Low-carb, Low-fat | £6.99 | |
| Best Food Fast | £6.99 | | Low-fat Feasts | £6.99 | |
| Best Food Mains | £6.99 | | Low-fat Food For Life | £6.99 | |
| Cakes, Biscuits & Slices | £6.99 | | Low-fat Meals in Minutes | £6.99 | |
| Cakes Cooking Class | £6.99 | | Main Course Salads | £6.99 | |
| Caribbean Cooking | £6.99 | | Middle Eastern Cooking Class | £6.99 | |
| Casseroles | £6.99 | | Midweek Meals in Minutes | £6.99 | |
| Chicken | £6.99 | | Muffins, Scones & Breads | £6.99 | |
| Chicken Meals in Minutes | £6.99 | | New Casseroles | £6.99 | |
| Chinese Cooking Class | £6.99 | | New Classics | £6.99 | |
| Christmas Cooking | £6.99 | | New Finger Food | £6.99 | |
| Chocolate | £6.99 | | Party Food and Drink | £6.99 | |
| Cocktails | £6.99 | | Pasta Meals in Minutes | £6.99 | |
| Cooking for Friends | £6.99 | | Potatoes | £6.99 | |
| Creative Cooking on a Budget | £6.99 | | Salads: Simple, Fast & Fresh | £6.99 | |
| Detox | £6.99 | | Saucery | £6.99 | |
| Dinner Beef | £6.99 | | Sauces, Salsas & Dressings (May '06) | £6.99 | |
| Dinner Lamb | £6.99 | | Sensational Stir-Fries | £6.99 | |
| Dinner Seafood | £6.99 | | Short-order Cook | £6.99 | |
| Easy Australian Style | £6.99 | | Slim | £6.99 | |
| Easy Curry | £6.99 | | Sweet Old-fashioned Favourites | £6.99 | |
| Easy Spanish-Style | £6.99 | | Thai Cooking Class | £6.99 | |
| Essential Soup | £6.99 | | Vegetarian Meals in Minutes | £6.99 | |
| Freezer, Meals from the | £6.99 | | Vegie Food | £6.99 | |
| French Food, New | £6.99 | | Weekend Cook | £6.99 | |
| Fresh Food for Babies & Toddlers | £6.99 | | Wicked Sweet Indulgences | £6.99 | |
| Get Real, Make a Meal | £6.99 | | Wok Meals in Minutes | £6.99 | |
| Good Food Fast | £6.99 | | TOTAL COST: | £ | |

Mr/Mrs/Ms _____

Address _____

_____ Postcode _____

Day time phone _____ Email* (optional) _____

I enclose my cheque/money order for £ _____

or please charge £ _____

to my: ☐ Access  ☐ Mastercard  ☐ Visa  ☐ Diners Club

PLEASE NOTE: WE DO NOT ACCEPT SWITCH OR ELECTRON CARDS

Card number ☐☐☐☐ ☐☐☐☐ ☐☐☐☐ ☐☐☐☐

Expiry date _____ 3 digit security code *(found on reverse of card)* _____

Cardholder's name_____ Signature _____

**To order:** Mail or fax – photocopy or complete the order form above, and send your credit card details or cheque payable to: Australian Consolidated Press (UK), Moulton Park Business Centre, Red House Road, Moulton Park, Northampton NN3 6AQ, phone (+44) (0) 1604 497531 fax (+44) (0) 1604 497533, e-mail books@acpmedia.co.uk or order online at www.acpuk.com
**Non-UK residents:** We accept the credit cards listed on the coupon, or cheques, drafts or International Money Orders payable in sterling and drawn on a UK bank. Credit card charges are at the exchange rate current at the time of payment.
**Postage and packing UK:** Add £1.00 per order plus 50p per book.
**Postage and packing overseas:** Add £2.00 per order plus £1.00 per book.
All pricing current at time of going to press and subject to change/availability.
**Offer ends 31.12.2006**

* By including your email address, you consent to receipt of any email regarding this magazine, and other emails which inform you of ACP's other publications, products, services and events, and to promote third party goods and services you may be interested in.